SEALIFE IN
JERSEY

A little souvenir by Sue Daly

CHRIS ANDREWS PUBLICATIONS

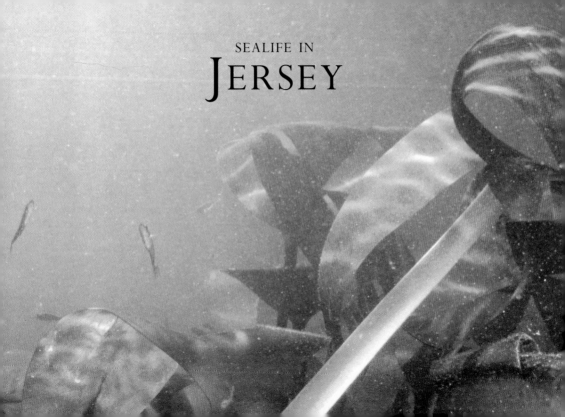

SEALIFE IN
JERSEY

The seas around Jersey are subject to one of the largest tidal movements on earth. Twice daily Atlantic waters surge through the English Channel and are amplified as they reflect back off the coast of France to the south and east of the island. When the gravitational pull of the moon is strongest the difference between high and low water can be as much as twelve metres. These are known as ormering tides in Jersey for it is then that the sea retreats far enough for people to gather a local delicacy. Found only around the Channel Islands and the adjacent coast of France, the name of this large shellfish is derived from *oreille de mer*, French for 'ear of the sea', because of its shape. The meat is treasured for ormer casserole and the beautiful mother-of-pearl lined shells can be seen decorating the walls of local gardens.

While the large tidal movements are good for shore gatherers, combined with the presence of so many rocks, they make the seas around Jersey a mariner's nightmare. The seabed is littered with wrecks, many of which date back to the grim days of the German occupation of the Channel Islands in the Second World War. In more recent times there has a been a programme of

Diver exploring the wreckage of a Second World War Dakota

controlled sinkings to create man-made reefs. However the ships find their way to the seabed, these un-natural offerings from the world above the waves are quickly colonised by sealife and make fascinating places to dive when the tide allows.

For marine life, the huge tidal movements are essential, carrying as they do masses of plankton, the tiny plants and animals that are the source of all life in the sea.

The other great influence on the marine life is Jersey's geographical position. Bathed in the warming current of the Gulf Stream, the island's southerly location means that, as on land, there is a rich mixture of wildlife under the waves. Sea creatures from the north thrive alongside those from much further south. This makes Jersey a fascinating place for anyone

Undulate Ray

with an interest in marine biology, be it professional or those armed simply with a bucket and fishing net. The rock pools are teeming with sea creatures from crabs, prawns and fishes to the less obvious sponges and sea squirts. Beyond the low tide line cuttlefish stalk their prey while seahorses and pipefish stay hidden among the seaweeds. In deeper water the granite walls are encrusted with colourful anemones and home to corals as delicate and beautiful as any found in tropical waters. Urchins and starfish graze among the boulders and down in the shingle flat fish lie in wait for a meal.

I have been photographing this wonderful marine life for almost twenty years and the pictures in this book represent just a fraction of the fascinating wealth of creatures living in the seas around Jersey. I hope this books inspires in the reader the same sense of wonder and privilege I feel to live surrounded by these maritime treasures and my concern that these seas remain some of the cleanest in Europe.

Bloody Henry starfish

Les Écréhous, a stunning reef off the north east coast

Gathering food from the seashore has been a tradition in Jersey for centuries. All sorts of implements have been designed for racking shellfish from the sand, hooking crabs and lobsters from their holes and prising ormers off the rocks. On the south east coast these arts have been taken a step further by those who have become farmers of the sea. Mussels are nurtured in graceful spirals around ten foot high poles and oysters grow inside mesh bags on low lying tables. Tending these crops requires an intimate knowledge of the tide because for much of the day the farmers' 'land' is underwater. The shellfish produced are grown without chemicals or fertilisers and, along with the local practice of diving for scallops, is a wonderful example of harvesting the ocean sustainably. If all fishing were done this way there really would be plenty more fish in the sea.

Mussels

Oyster Tables

12   Japweed, an alien invader from the Pacific which first arrived in the 1980s

Elephant's Hide Sponge and Painted Topshell

14   Yellow Staghorn Sponge

Sponge

Sponges and anemones live in many of the marine habitats around Jersey from the shallows to the deeper waters. Some have even evolved to cope with life in the harsh world between the tides. Sponges feed by drawing water through their pores and filtering out tiny particles of food. They grow in a variety of shapes from flat cushions and lobes to strange spikes and fingers. Anemones all share a basic form; a mouth circled by stinging tentacles. To us the stings are harmless but to a small creature venturing too close they are deadly.

Jewel Anemones

Snakelocks Anemone

18   Elegant Anemones

Yellow Cluster Anemones

Marine worms occur in a variety of different shapes and sizes, each adapted to its environment. Tube worms secrete a leathery tube to protect their soft bodies. A whorl of tentacles blossoms from the top gathering particles of food for the animal which are passed down to its stomach. Flat worms have very thin bodies with two distinct tentacles at the head end. Corals are also a very diverse group of animals and their presence in such cool waters is often a surprise. Unlike their tropical relatives, those that live in Jersey, at least eight species, are not dependent on sunlight. Instead they catch particles of food in their tentacles. Fan and soft corals are colonial where as cup corals live as solitary polyps.

Double Spiral Worm

Peacock Tube Worms

Candy-striped Flatworm feeding on Light Bulb Sea Squirts

Devonshire Cup Corals live as solitary polyps emerging from a hard cup

Jersey's north coast in autumn

25

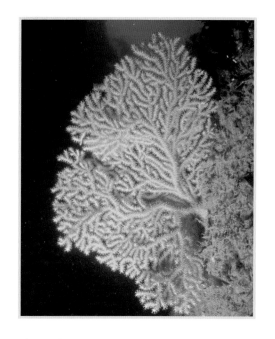

26   Fan Coral

Dogfish egg on Fan Coral

The feeding polyps of Red Sea Fingers Soft Coral

Lobsters and crabs have been the mainstay of Jersey's fishing industry for centuries. In the past the pots to trap them were made of willow and were raised and lowered by hand. They were fragile so fishing only took place in summer. With the development of sturdy plastic and steel pots and the use of mechanical winches, fishing is now a year round business. Boats are able to fish a thousand pots a day and electronic navigation equipment allows them to be placed in exactly the best spots. To preserve the valuable stocks restrictions are placed on the industry, particularly on the design of the pots themselves. All the same, the tonnage of lobster alone taken from Channel Island waters every year amounts to more than half of that captured around Wales and England together. Fortunately for lobsters, the rocky Island waters are among the richest in the world for the species so, with continued careful management, both fishermen and lobsters can survive.

Crabs, prawns and lobsters all share the characteristic of having a soft body protected by a hard shell and each species has evolved to live in a slightly different way. Squat Lobsters live in narrow cracks so have flattened bodies and claws. Hermit Crabs have no shell on the back half of their bodies so live in abandoned seashells to protect their vulnerable soft tails.

Squat Lobster

Lobster

Squat Lobster

Hermit Crab photographed while changing shell with soft tail exposed

32   Edible Crab, more commonly known in Jersey as the Chancre Crab

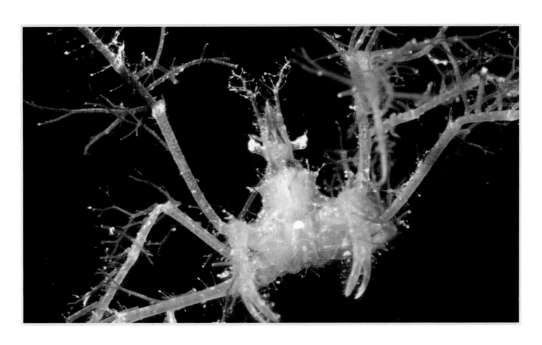

Scorpion Spider Crab, tiny at just 2cm across its body

34 Male Velvet Swimming Crab guarding his female until she is ready to mate

This tiny prawn is immune to the anemone's sting and lives among its tentacles unharmed

36   Just some of the seashells to be found on Jersey's shores

A scallop faces into the tide to feed on particles of food in the current

38 The Ormer, a type of abalone, grazes on red seaweeds

Pennant's Topshells, a southern species not found on the shores of mainland Britain

St Ouen's Bay on the west coast

41

Sea slugs fall into two different groups. Sea Hares have a delicate internal shell and eject bright purple ink when disturbed. Some years huge numbers of these hand-sized creatures strand on the shore. Nudibranchs are smaller and often very brightly coloured with elaborate tentacles. All are hermaphrodites, each individual having both male and female organs. This means that every sea slug they encounter of the same species is a potential mate, thereby doubling their chances of reproducing.

Crystal Sea Slug

44   Nudibranch feeding on hydroids

Yellow Edged Nudibranchs mating

Although all fish have fins, tails, eyes and a mouth, each species has developed a unique shape and colour to suit its lifestyle. There are over a hundred species in the waters around Jersey from tiny Seahorses to enormous Conger Eels. In winter many move to deeper, less turbulent water off-shore returning to the shallows in spring to breed.

Some have elaborate courtship rituals which can involve males building a nest or changing colour to attract a mate. By summer the rock pools, sandy bays and kelp-covered reefs are teeming with fish.

Streaked Gurnard

Short-snouted Seahorse

John Dory

50   The Black-face Blenny is a southern species rarely found around the British mainland

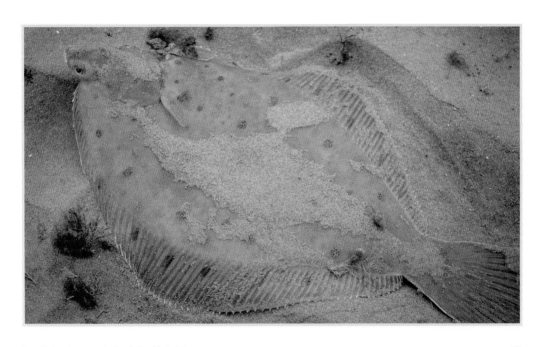

The Plaice is the only flat fish with bright orange spots

Compass Jellyfish

Barrel Jellyfish

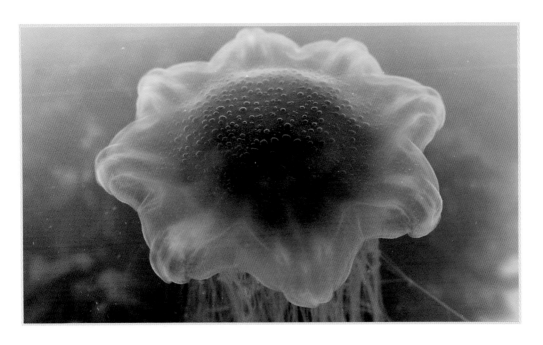

Lion's Mane Jellyfish

Sea Squirts are often mistaken for some kind of plant growth but are in fact quite complex animals. They begin life drifting in the plankton in larval form, like tiny tadpoles, and have a simple backbone and nerve cord. When they settle and develop into adults these are lost but indicate a strong connection to those of us from a more advanced form of life.

Some sea squirts live a solitary life while others, like those on these pages, form colonies with many individuals living joined together. Each one pumps water into its intestine where tiny particles of food are filtered out before the used water is expelled. If disturbed the body contracts rapidly and squirts out any water inside, hence their name.

Light Bulb Sea Squirts

Corbière Lighthouse

57

58 Cuttlefish displaying stripes

Although cuttlefish and starfish share the same four letters at the end of their name, neither are fish nor are they related to each other. Cuttlefish belong to the mollusc family which also contains slugs and snails. Cuttlefish are very intelligent with large brains, excellent eyesight and a remarkable ability to change not only colour but texture in an instant. This, combined with their lightning speed, makes them formidable predators quite capable of catching and eating prey larger than themselves. Starfish are echinoderms, a family also containing urchins and sea cucumbers. They share a radial symmetry with five sections, although the Sunstar is the exception to this rule with anything between eight and twelve arms. Starfish have the amazing ability to regenerate lost limbs and a single arm can grow a whole new starfish if part of the central body is still attached.

Cuttlefish eating a Dragonet

60   The Sunstar, one of the largest starfish in Jersey's waters

The tiny Cushion Star, just 5cm across, is found in rock pools

Common Urchin with tube feet extended

Produced by Chris Andrews Publications

Tel: +44(0)1865 723404 email: chris.andrews1@btclick.com **www: cap-ox.com**

In association with Gateway Publishing Ltd Sark

ISBN 978-1-905385-66-9

Photographed by Sue Daly with Chris Andrews. Text Sue Daly.

Front Cover: Grève De Lecq with sealife Back Cover: Cuttlefish and diver

Title Page: Short-snouted Seahorse